RIO GRANDE
MOUNTAINS
TO THE SEA

RIO GRANDE
MOUNTAINS TO THE SEA

PHOTOGRAPHS BY JIM BONES

TexasMonthlyPress

Texas Monthly Press, Inc.
P.O. Box 1569
Austin, Texas 78767

A   B   C   D   E   F   G   H

Library of Congress Cataloging in Publication Data

Bones, Jim
    Rio Grande Mountains to the sea.

    1. Rio Grande Valley—Description and travel—Views.
2. Rio Grande—Description and travel—Views.
I. Title.
F392.R5B66   1985   976.4′4   85–2849
ISBN 0-87719-008-9

Printed in Japan by
Dai Nippon Printing Co. LTD.
through DNP (America), Inc.

Frontispiece

Evening thunderstorm over the Rio Grande
Valley in New Mexico

Design by
The Smitherman Corporation

*This book is dedicated
with love to my son, Paul Daniel,
who began life by this river,
with the hope that it helps save a little wild space
where children may always find peace.*

I believe in a Supreme Power, unknowable and impersonal, whose hand-iwork the soul-enlarging firmament declares. However, I believe in question-ings, doubtings, searchings, skepticism, and I discredit credulity, or blind faith. The progress of man is based on disbelief of the commonly accepted. The noblest minds and natures of human history have thought and sung, lived and died, trying to budge the status quo toward a larger and fuller status. I am sustained by a belief in evolution—the "increasing purpose" of life in which the rational is with geological slowness evolving out of the irrational. To believe that goodness and wisdom and righteousness in Garden of Eden perfection lie somewhere far ahead instead of farther and farther behind gives me hope and somewhat explains existence. This is a long view. I do not pretend that it is always present in me. It does raise me when I have it, however. . .

For me the beautiful resides in the physical, but it is spiritual. I have never heard a sermon as spiritual in either phrase or fact as "Waters on a starry night are beautiful and free."

J. Frank Dobie

ACKNOWLEDGMENTS

Hundreds of wonderful people helped make this book a reality, and I thank them all for their contributions large and small. I am particularly grateful to Suzanne Winckler, who saved the book more than once from editorial disaster, and to Marshall Johnston, Bill Muehlberger, Russell Lee, and John Graves, who shared their knowledge of biology, geology, photography, and human nature with me. I owe a great deal to the care and consideration of Ann Matlock, with whom I first explored the distant reaches of this river. I am pleased to have learned the skills of river running from my compadres David Hollingsworth, Steve Harris, Michael Davidson, Catfish Callaway, and John D'Anna. I was sustained throughout this long endeavor by the dear members of my adopted family—Kirk Bonds, Cindy Cary, Steve Catron, Harold and Denise Crawford, Richard Davis, Dwight Deal, Hal and Mary Flanders, Warren Hanford, Vickie Harris, Kathy Heidel, Todd and Ruth Ann Jagger, Jimmy Jalapeeno, Edgar Kincaid, Tracy Lynch, Alan Masters, Chris McCarthy, Gath Anna Parmenas, Tahmina Shalizi and Nick Potter, Nancy Jane Reid, Devi and Hunter Sharp, Ken Smith, and Max Thomas— and my own mother, Nell, my father, Jim, my brother, Robert, and his wife, Stephanie. Finally, with the steady love and encouragement of Laura Lee and Karen Copeland, I have been able to complete this work.

INTRODUCTION

Rivers run full of paradox, beginning at their ends, so to speak, remaking the lands they flow through on their way from the mountains to the sea. Some geologists say rivers are ephemeral phenomena, of insignificant and short-lived duration, but collectively rivers have wasted all the high places of the former continents back into the ocean's cradle. Out of the seas from which they are born, rivers are continually distilled by the sun into clouds that flow like rivers themselves on prevailing winds over mountains and valleys, deserts and plains, that constantly change as well.

Mountains too are born and grow and die. They flow, grain by grain, just as rivers do, and both owe their existence to a restless planet, alive with internal forces. When land rises above sea level, and shorelines recede, then water runs downhill as streams flow together, bound again for their source. The first places to drain are low coastal wetlands. Then, later, mountain basins overflow and enter older established channels. Most great rivers begin as several separate tributaries that gradually integrate, growing headward into unknown regions, in much the same way our lives are made of many different experiences.

The Rio Grande is an ancient family of rivers that join as they cross the continent, and each member has its own distinct history and appearance.

Spanish sailors who first saw the river named it Rio de las Palmas for the groves of native palm trees that once filled its lower delta. Then the Rio Pecos was discovered on the dry Texas plains, wandering along the edge of the Despoblado. Later, conquistadores charted what they called the Rio Bravo del Norte as it flowed from Colorado through the long valley of New Mexico. Finally, traders crossing Chihuahua found the river that they named the Rio Conchos, "river of shells," for the fossils in its bed. When, during the last hundred years, people came to realize that it was actually all one system, the name was enlarged to Rio Grande, great river of destiny.

Although it gathers waters in two large nations—from the states of Colorado, New Mexico, Texas, Chihuahua, Durango, Coahuila, Nuevo León, and Tamaulipas—the Rio Grande is composed of only twenty major streams. Flowing south from the United States, they are the Rios Bravo, Conejos, Costilla, Rojo, Chama, Jemez, Puerco, Pecos, and Diablo. Mexico contributes the Rios Conchos, Balleza, Parral, Florida, San Pedro, Chuvíscar, Salado, Sabinas, Salinas, Pesquira, and San Juan.

This widespread family, the third-longest drainage between Canada and Guatemala, traverses many geographic provinces as it flows 1885 miles from the continental divide to the Gulf of Mexico. Its two volcanic head-waters lie in the southern Rocky Mountains and the northern Sierra Madres. Both sources meet in the vast Big Bend, amid the tilted fault blocks of the Basin and Range. Together, they cross eroded plateaus at the tail end of the Great High Plains and finally wind over their own coastal delta that extends into the rolling maritime waves. On its long journey the Rio Grande encounters most of the major life zones in North America, from alpine tundra nearly three miles high through tall forests, dry savannahs, arid deserts, tropical thorn woods, and southern prairies all the way to low sandy shores. The river changes so often throughout its long body that there is much disagreement about its origins and forms.

A time-lapse film spanning millions of years would show the Rio Grande flickering in and out of existence, dancing about migrating head-waters, from first earthly uplift to final surrender. But human thinking tends to be linear, perhaps because of the way we string words together, so many people believe that a river simply starts at one place, then flows to another. A river, however, is really a cyclic being and encompasses events that span vast time and space. Things that happened billions of years ago still determine where and how a river rolls. Although a single moist thread in an alpine meadow may for convenience be called the beginning, a river rises all at once over several wide basins and, like truth, never ends but flows on forever.

I fell in love with the Rio Grande because of a dream that repeatedly told me if I wanted to know the secrets of my own being, I must go first to the mountains and then to the sea. For the past twenty years, as I walked, rode, and floated throughout the Rio Grande's home country, I discovered that rivers cut to the very heart of things, of rock and life and even dreams. I learned that dreams, like rivers, are themselves paradoxical, being as real to the mind as anything can be. They are very much alike in substance and effect, and both create pathways to be retraced to the same primal source.

My long friend has taught me to treasure the wild free spaces in which life goes on unimpeded and those special rare places where no one has marked the rocks or defiled the wellsprings of personal experience. I found that what I am after, if truth be known, is the individual ecstasy of a natural revelation that joins me directly to the land I live on.

How you envision the very beginning of things is purely an act of personal faith. I have no difficulty believing that the Starmaker, with infinite patience and cosmic intelligence, called forth the universe in a burst of brilliant light. From there it is a simple sequence of matter's condensing into elements, galaxies, and suns, with planets whirling round in various forms. The exact genesis is relatively unimportant, because we know by experience that the world really exists, but our innate curiosity compels us to search for the story of how it all happened.

According to gathered speculation, the earth first took shape in the Hadean Eon, less than five billion years ago, from an amorphous association of stellar dust swept out of space by waves of gravity playing through our young solar system. Drawn together by matter's eternal longing for itself, particles coalesced to form a homogeneous body that ever so gradually compressed. Heated with internal atomic decay, battered by huge meteorites, and strained from tidal friction, metallic elements finally reached a critical point of phase change about four billion years before present, and the infant planet underwent a great metamorphism. In a cataclysmic upheaval of fire and steam, unequaled in worldly evolution, primordial crust disintegrated, overturned, and melted. At the same time, iron became molten and collapsed to the center of the fractionating earth, while less dense molecular aggregates rose.

During this so-called Iron Catastrophe, a substantial atmosphere was released for the first time and abundant water vapor was expelled from crucibles deep within, where minerals were being forged. Small rafts of lighter residue may have moved freely about the fluid surface and collected at the convergence of huge interior convective cells generated by migrating iron. These fragments, combined and remelted in the presence of juvenile gases, may have expanded to form the seeds of cratons and the roots of ancestral continents.

After cooling sufficiently, a new crust thickened with granitic pieces embedded in its surface, and a rudimentary ocean precipitated from global storms of unparalleled intensity. With this loss of heat came shrinkage, primitive mountains emerged, and the earliest rivers ran from the barren peaks to desolate shores, carrying salts and sediments to the prenatal sea.

For the next billion years, as the young earth spun on through the Archean Eon, it underwent changes marked only by twisted clues in metamorphic stone, and the earliest traces of life were preserved. During this time the brittle crust eventually grew rigid, and then, more than two billion years ago, in the Proterozoic Eon, it apparently broke into a mosaic of huge plates that began to move about the suboceanic surface, driven by immense convective currents still churning within. Great rifts formed as crustal pieces pulled apart and dense molten rock welled up from the interior to spread across widening sea floors, only to be dragged down again along cooler subduction zones where colliding plates descended. Lighter granitic continental masses remained isostatically higher, refusing to be taken into the subterranean cauldrons. Consequently, these continents enlarged at their margins as new land was sutured on and great mountains were raised, then weathered away. Throughout the turbulent Proterozoic Eon, while pieces of crustal puzzle joined and parted, consuming old oceans and opening others, abundant fossils appeared, first as one-celled algae, followed much later by tiny invertebrate animals. Between 600 and 300 million years ago in the Paleozoic Era, as vertebrates developed and terrestrial life forms moved inland, the plates reassembled to rise as the most recent supercontinent, Pangaea, surrounded by a global sea, Panthalassa.

During the creation of Pangaea, the ancient Atlantic Ocean slowly closed as North America and Africa were sutured together, causing the main Appalachians and ancestral Rockies to rise. At essentially the same time, South America jammed Yucatán into the Gulf of Mexico, and the eastern Sierra Madre first uplifted as part of the Ouachita Orogeny. For almost 200 million years a single landmass existed, while reptiles grew huge, small mammals appeared, tall forests spread, and the mountains gradually eroded. About 180 million years back, in the Mesozoic Era, Pangaea ruptured, the modern Atlantic reopened, North America's Great Western Basin lifted slightly, and the Sierra Nevada began to show.

North America drifted westward away from the widening Mid-Atlantic Rift, a process that went on mostly unimpeded into the Cretaceous Period, as shallow seas invaded the heartland and laid down sheets of fossiliferous limestone. Then, about 100 million years ago, like a huge brittle carpet sliding across a floor, our continent collided with the Farallon Plate in the northeastern Pacific Basin. So mighty was the impact that North America compressed and rode over the Pacific bottom, driving it deep under the continental platform, deforming the basement rock.

During the Laramide Orogeny, North America continued to grind over the descending plate, causing the continent to arch upward and inland seas to retreat. Sporadically, with intense folding and thrust faulting along old cratonic boundaries, a long spine buckled into the sky from Alaska to Mexico, forming the Great Divide. These rising mountains intercepted moisture-laden winds off the Pacific Ocean and, through precipitation, began to create rivers, including the ancestral Rio Grande. They also made wide rain shadows on their lee sides, which eventually led to the formation of deserts throughout the western third of the continent. The tectonic upheavals of the Cenozoic Era that commenced about 65 million years ago were accompanied by a revolution of life. Conifers, ferns, and their allies declined as modern flowering plants flourished along with quickly adaptive insects. The great age of reptiles abruptly ended. Birds and mammals became ascendant on the land, and bony fishes grew dominant in the seas.

Erosion replaced deposition as soon as land began to rise above the waves, so the Tertiary headwaters of the Rio Grande underwent dissection even as they were being born. Because of their close proximity to the Gulf Basin, the streams of the Sierra Madre Oriental probably established the first connecting drainages across the plains of Texas, Tamaulipas, Nuevo León, and Coahuila, through the ancestral Rios San Juan, Sabinas, and Salado. Continued integration may next have added the waters of the ancestral Rios

Pecos from New Mexico and Conchos from Chihuahua, followed by those of the Rio Bravo from as far away as Arizona and Colorado. Whatever the exact evolution, throughout the Paleocene Epoch a major river system grew, and it must have been magnificent, for it carried heavy resistant quartzite pebbles all the way from the continental divide to the Gulf of Mexico.

In the Eocene Epoch, perhaps 50 million years before present, late-maturing ranges began turning northern-flowing streams south and westward. The structures of the lower reaches of the river, from about Langtry south, were little affected by these distant events, but the river itself suffered indirectly. It was deprived of sustaining waters, and sedimentary deposition decreased in the Rio Grande Embayment.

By 40 million years ago most of the proud peaks of the early cordillera had died, planed down to rolling high country by all the brown rivers that gnawed at their sides. Again in the Oligocene Epoch, about 30 million years back, renewed uplift occurred as the melted distillates of the subducted Farallon Plate intruded and exploded through the crust. As they escaped, gaseous magmas spread thick ash and lava flows over the older compressional structures and built extensive volcanoes throughout the tortured West. With this uplift, overall stream flows increased for a while, then became intermittent as the young volcanic rocks created immense barriers that impounded or further diverted sections of the venerable upper river. During this epoch, thousands of feet of new crust were added to the aging highlands of the Rio Grande in the Rocky Mountains and Sierra Madres.

Tertiary volcanism began to abate after North America completely extinguished the old Farallon Plate. In the early Miocene Epoch, about 25 million years ago, the continent pushed over the East Pacific Rise and collided with the tail end of the westward-growing Pacific Plate, and massive rifting began. Tectonic processes were suddenly—in terms of geologic time—reversed, and North America from the Rockies to the Pacific Coast was wrenched apart westward as the Colorado Plateau and High Plains began to separate.

When compressional forces relaxed, the crust extended by at least forty miles and cracked into north-south trending horsts and grabens that alternately rose and fell like great stone waves, in what is called the Basin and Range block-faulting episode. Whatever remained of the Rio Grande's original through-flowing drainage vanished into the chaos of the bolson valleys that subsided as the continent began to open. Only the lower reaches of the former river channel below Del Rio survived relatively intact, and for about 20 million years this part of the river awaited eventual reunion with its northern family of streams.

Throughout the Miocene Epoch and into the Pliocene, sporadic volcanic activity continued while grabens fell and horst blocks rose. As flash floods eroded the rising edges of the horst blocks, they carried deposits of coarsely sorted conglomerates into intervening bolsons that contained intermittent playa lakes, and this accumulating sediment caused the waters to rise. For 20 million years or so, individual tributaries wandered the cordillera from basin to basin, filling them, then spilling through passes in different directions, at times reuniting, then parting again, in response to earth movements that have yet to end.

Back when North America separated from Pangaea in the Mesozoic Era, it lay nearer the equator and enjoyed a more moderate climate. By the end of the Cenozoic Era, however, it had drifted closer to the North Pole and become much cooler. Perhaps due to a combination of events, such as decline of solar energy, worldwide rise of great mountain chains, and restricted circulation of arctic seas, more snow began to fall in winter than could ever melt in summer. For whatever reasons, between the Pliocene and Pleistocene epochs, the global temperature plummeted and massive ice sheets began grinding like mobile rocks from the polar regions across the temperate zones.

In four great surges, continental glaciers extended as far south as Kentucky and Missouri, while alpine ice fields crowned the higher western mountains from Colorado and California to Canada. After each advance the ice retreated, melting back toward the pole, sending incredible volumes of water coursing down the valleys it had gouged. Each interglacial episode helped fill the remaining closed basins of the upper Rio Grande. One by one they spilled over, sending the river closer to the Gulf of Mexico.

Glaciers never lay on the headwaters of the Rio Conchos, but they grew as close as New Mexico, and their cold breath spread heavy rains and snow deep into the Sierra Madres. Since the Rio Conchos was able to flow nearly year-round, it probably reestablished a through-flowing drainage before the Rio Bravo did, but the Rio Pecos, which ran from lower, less-broken country, probably preceded them both in doing so. Some time in the past two million years, the Rio Bravo del Norte finally overflowed its most southern basins, rolling through the growing desert to join the Rio Conchos in the Big Bend region and rediscover a path down ancestral canyons to the waiting arms of the sea.

As Pleistocene glaciers receded, *Homo sapiens* began invading this formerly uninhabited continent. Along with herds of strange woolly animals in sweeping migrations, they poured over this newfound land. It was the beginning of the Psychozoic Era, which brought the flame of self-awareness to our ancestors and also unleashed the greatest force for planetary change in the history of life on earth. Ten thousand years ago these paleolithic hunters may have actually driven huge herds of post-Pleistocene creatures over the edge of extinction. Armed with stone points and raging fires, they forever tipped the balance of evolution. But the alterations caused by early Indians, profound as they were, cannot compare to the accelerated changes we have wrought in the last century of industrialization.

Even though the Rio Grande has been occupied by people for millennia, in only one hundred years most of its virgin forests have been lumbered, its tall grasses badly stripped, its fertile soils plundered, and its remaining wild creatures mercilessly hunted. In just fifty years its waters have nearly all been sucked dry and its accessible minerals ripped from the earth. Like a gigantic crazed beast tearing its body apart, we have destroyed the river's finest treasures. With plows and guns, mines and sawmills, dams and highways, and greedy ignorance, we have roared right up to the great divide of life itself.

Below Oscura Peak, at the end of the Jornada del Muerto—dead ancestral valley of the Rio Grande—the first atomic bomb was exploded forty years ago. With that detonation near Socorro, the great river witnessed the awesome glow of what may be the darkest event in human memory. That unparalleled loss of innocence brought the ability to annihilate not only ourselves but perhaps all other life as well. Even if we manage to escape that fate, our race for the "good life" promises to poison the soil, water, and air, which sustain us, before the next generation dies of old age.

The river itself is an excellent indicator of the relative health of our environment. Impounded, diverted, polluted, abused, consumed in countless ways, it now approaches a state of terminal decay. And since all rivers are really the roots of the oceans, whatever befalls them involves the whole world. The prospects are none too good at this moment, for if the mineral-bearing rivers fail to nourish the seas, which cradle the one-celled algae that make the oxygen you and I breathe, we will all perish.

It is tragically ironic, considering the geologic antiquity of this planet, that a single species of its multibillion-year-old biota holds the fate of all life in its clever little hands. Which way will we turn, I now wonder. The choice is urgent and entirely our own, but the consequences may determine the future of life forever. I, for one, pray that my child has the chance to follow his own dreams and discover the world of tomorrow filled with beautiful wonders and secret wild places where living rivers still run from the mountains to the sea.

Jim Bones
Santa Fe, New Mexico

COLORADO
NEW MEXICO

N

San Juan Mts
Sangre de Cristo Mts
Spring Pass
San Luis Valley
Great Sand Dunes
Taos Plateau Bridge
Rio Chama
Jemez Mts
Santa Fe
Albuquerque
Rio Grande
Socorro
Rio Pecos
Guadalupe Mts
Tularosa Basin
White Sands
Jornado del Muerto
El Paso
Mimbres Mts
NEW

0   20   40   60
10   30   50   70
Miles
Scale

Reprinted by permission of Robert C. Belcher, Baylor Geological Studies,
1975, Bulletin 29, Geomorphic Evolution of the Rio Grande

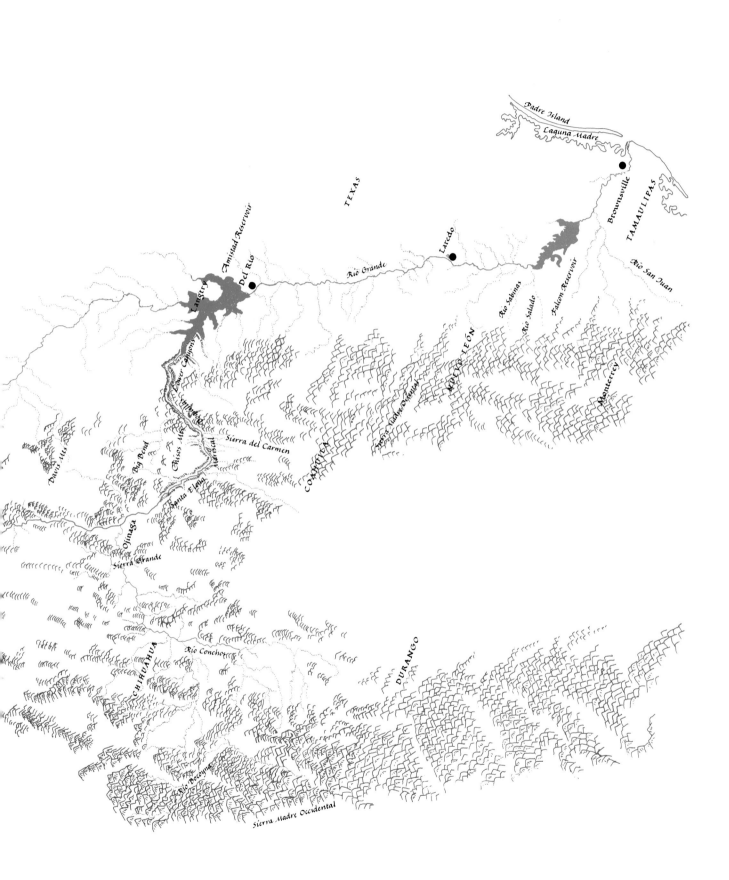

Padre Island

Laguna Madre

TEXAS

Brownsville

TAMAULIPAS

Amistad Reservoir

Del Rio

LanSin

Laredo

Rio Grande

Rio San Juan

Rio Sabinas

Rio Salado

Falcon Reservoir

NUEVO LEÓN

Lower Canyons

Sierra Madre Oriental

Carmen Mts

Sierra del Carmen

COAHUILA

Monterrey

Davis Mts

Big Bend

Chisos Mts

Mariscal

Santa Elena

Ojinaga

Sierra Grande

CHIHUAHUA

Rio Conchos

DURANGO

Rio Bocoyna

Sierra Madre Occidental

19

RIO GRANDE
MOUNTAINS TO THE SEA

Full moon over Indian Ridge

Beartown, the site of several abandoned mines, lies in the shadows beneath the ridge on the banks of Bear Creek, one of the three main headwater forks of the Rio Grande.

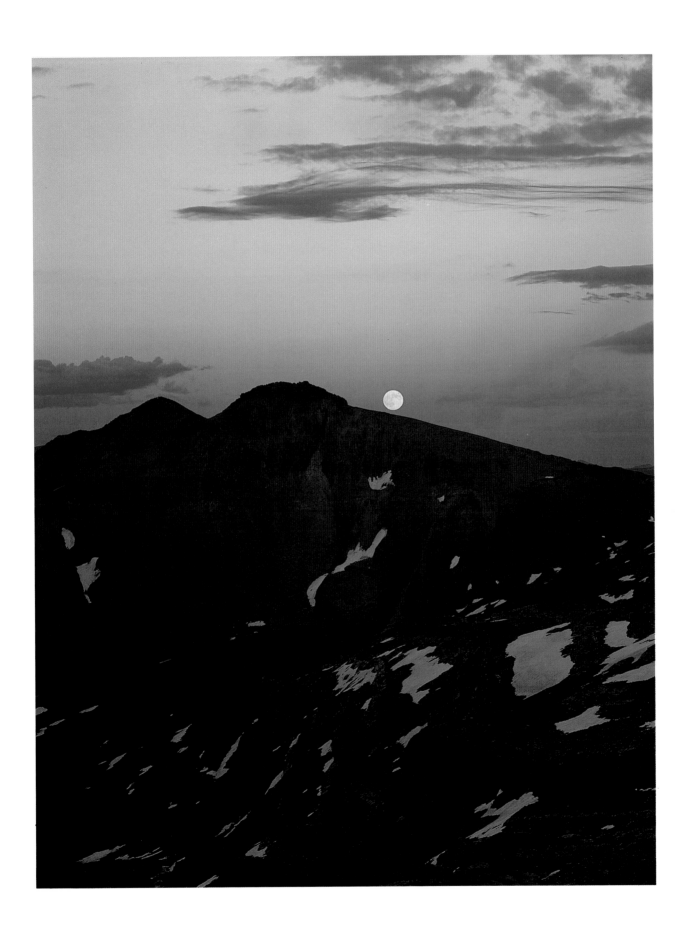

Slate at Kite Lake

This rock was deposited as quiescent ocean sediment more than 600 million years ago, then raised by repeated mountain-building episodes. Exposed by erosion, it is slowly returning to the sea. Growing in the fractures of the stone are cinquefoil and a plant called kinnikinnick, or bearberry.

San Juan Dome from Stony Pass

On the horizon, beyond the fields of gold
autumn tundra, are the 14,000-foot needle
peaks of the Grenadier Range. On the
southwestern boundary of the Rio Grande
headwaters, they are the highest part
of the volcanic uplift that formed
the ancestral river.

The infant Rio Grande near Timber Hill

Just above Timber Hill the streams and creeks and rills of the headwaters first come together as a recognizable river, and the Rio Grande now attains the force to erode the complex rock into the first cobbles and boulders. In essence, two rivers are born on these mountains, the river of water and the river of stone.

Sunrise on clouds

During a break in an autumn snowstorm,
the clouds rose up from the valley of the
Rio Grande to the surrounding peaks. It
was almost as if the breath of the mountains
were being exhaled at dawn.

Beaver lodge and pond

Beavers enforce part of the ecological succession in the high country when they dam up a stream for their lodge. A small lake forms, which over time clogs with debris dropped by the water, and that in turn forms a moist meadow where the aspens and firs can grow.

Midwinter in the upper Rio Grande Valley

Until April, when the snows begin to
melt, this point near the Rio Grande
Reservoir is as far up into the headwaters
as you can go.

South Fork of the Rio Grande

A record of each storm is preserved in the
fringe of snow along the riverbank—the
snow blows in, and then, during the days
of clear weather, the sun crystallizes the
surface and forms a crust, which becomes
the floor for the next storm. The snow
holds another record: the tracks of an
animal, possibly a ferret, that explored
each vale in the snow, until it finally found
a crossing.

A seep in winter

A headwater seep is locked up until spring,
its flow immobilized into icicles and glassy
housing for last season's flower stalks and
grasses.

Roseroot near Stony Pass

This seep, above timberline and on the continental divide, is blanketed with flowers in summer. Roseroot is a rare succulent that grows in rocky alpine niches in northwestern America and eastern Asia. Marsh marigold, the white flower, is more common in alpine areas.

*Western slope of the continental divide
from Stony Pass*

Looking like a crumpled sheet of paper,
these mountains are the remains of the San
Juan Dome, originally built up from the ash
and lava of a series of volcanoes. The whole
structure collapsed into a group of calderas
when underground magma chambers
emptied. It was subsequently covered by
more eruptions and then carved by glaciers
into sharp peaks and rounded alpine slopes.

Swift water on the South Fork
of the Rio Grande

The concavity in the water is called a hole,
a hydraulic event that occurs when water
falling over a boulder or ledge tries to flow
fast enough to keep up with the rest of the
stream around it.

44

North Clear Creek Falls

This cascade, draining the northern part
of the Rio Grande headwaters, tumbles
over a lava rim into a ninety-foot chasm.
Carving its way through the rock, like a
saw cutting a piece of wood, the waterfall
demonstrates how rivers are formed through
headward erosion. Yellow monkey flowers
are scattered on the canyon wall to catch
the waterfall's mists.

Green aspen and Douglas fir,
near Pole Creek

Trees just below timberline grow bent and twisted from persistent winds and winter snows but flourish all the same in the brief warmth of summer.

Wheeler Geological Area

Pinnacles, hoodoos, and other strange
formations are weathering out of the
volcanic tuff so quickly that very little
vegetation can grow here. At 13,000 feet,
this is one of the highest deserts on earth.

Summer storm over Great Sand Dunes and Medano Pass

The spine of a dune is made and remade by the shifting winds. On the windward side of the dune they shove the sand into a crest, then tiny avalanches of sand cascade down the lee side, and in this way the winds slowly move the dunes around.

Rio Grande Gorge from Taos High Bridge

The gorge begins as a shallow canyon up near the Colorado border, but it gets deeper and deeper, reaching its maximum depth of a thousand feet near Taos. The river is low and clear now because it is autumn and the high country is beginning to freeze up.

Cottonwoods and willows
by the Rio Chama

The Chama, which represents about a
quarter of the headwaters, drains the
southern slopes of the San Juan Mountains
before it joins the Rio Grande at Española.

*Rocky creek in the Sangre
de Cristo Mountains*

This creek, lined with dense stands of
mountain ash, willow, and spruce, is typical
of the thousands of headwater streams in
the Rio Grande drainage.

First snowfall on aspens

By October, and the first snow, the aspens
have faded from their high yellows. Their
leaves will fall soon.

Rose hips in snow

The fruits are left over from the previous summer, covered and deep-frozen until about late April, when the snow begins to melt. In spring, they are the first offerings for birds.

Granite boulders covered by snow

Winter storms provide most of the moisture that fills the Rio Grande when spring thaws the high country.

Aspen and spruce in fog

By early June the aspens are barely greening in the mountains. This place is at the headwaters of the Rio Costilla, a major tributary of the Rio Grande that flows out of the northern Sangre de Cristos.

Blue columbine growing with elk thistle

The big powder-blue columbine, three inches across, blooms from June to the first hard freeze in moist high-country meadows.

Fallen logs in Nambe Lake, Sangre de Cristo Mountains

Winter winds often blow down the exposed timber that lines the alpine lakes, leaving the logs to bleach in the summer sun.

Sunset reflection in Nambe Lake

The flamelike light in the water comes from
the late sun shining on a bare cliff that rises
behind the lake. The wall is a cirque,
which bears the shape and imprints of an
old glacier.

Summer lightning over the
Rio Grande Valley

Frequent thunderstorms in July and August
stalk the upper watershed. They can cause
powerful flash floods and start forest fires.

Sandstone bluffs near Grants

When the sandstone was uplifted, it cracked into blocks, but they remained closely jointed. The surface was then exposed to rain, snow, and ice—which worked fastest at the joints, the weakest points in the sandstone. The erosion first formed fins, then the fins weathered down to these pillars. All the while, the wind polished, rounded, and sculpted the surfaces.

Permanent ice in a lava cave

Any water that runs into these underground chambers freezes and never thaws because the caves are at such a high altitude and the lava walls provide indomitable insulation.

Hot springs in the Jemez Mountains

The 110-degree water in this spring, one of
the many dozens of hot springs in the area,
is heated by an old volcanic vent. It is a
signal that the volcanoes in the Rio Grande
Rift region, though dormant, are not
extinct. The mountains are still rising and
the valleys falling, and someday the whole
area could reawaken.

Basalt boulders in Rio Grande Gorge

After spring floods subside and water on the riverside boulders evaporates, a coating of iron and manganese oxides remains on the basalt. This residue, which has a bluish-purple cast, is called desert varnish.

*Spring floodwaters at Catfish Falls,
Pecos River*

At this season the water comes in distinct
pulses—falling in the evening, rising
several feet by midmorning. These ebbs and
flows reflect the effect of the sun melting
snow in the high country. In 1980 Catfish
Falls was drowned behind Los Esteros Dam,
and the area is now a popular catfish lake.

A nest of red-tailed hawks on a Pecos River cliff

Parts of a kangaroo rat, a Great Plains skink, a rabbit, and a checkered garter snake—leftovers from feeding—lie strewn around the two redtail nestlings. The chick in the remaining egg has started to pip its way out.

Bosque del Apache National
Wildlife Refuge

This swampy woods between Las Cruces
and Socorro is a prime wintering spot for
ducks, geese, and, since the mid-seventies,
the endangered whooping crane. By placing
whooper eggs in the nests of sandhill cranes
at Grays Lake National Wildlife Refuge
in Idaho, biologists established another
whooping crane colony far removed from
the birds' other breeding place in Canada.
In winter this new flock, which numbers
thirty birds, migrates to Bosque del Apache.

Lava flow at Carrizozo, Valley of Fires

Winter grasses, hedgehog cactus, and cholla are growing on the basalt. The flow, which occurred about a thousand years ago, is probably the most recent flow in the Rio Grande watershed. Hawaiian terms are used to describe the form in which the lava hardened. The ropy rock that looks like chocolate pudding is called *pahoehoe*; the jagged, angular lava is called *aa*.

White Sands

White Sands, adjoining the Carrizozo lava flow, is in the Tularosa Basin. Fifty to a hundred bolsons similar to this one eventually integrated and became the through-flowing Rio Grande, but some, like the Tularosa, were never completely breached. Water collected in the basin, but only to evaporate. At the same time, runoff from the mountains deposited gypsum, which the wind now blows into dunes.

*Ponderosa pine and Gambel oak,
Mimbres Mountains*

This forest, in the southwest corner of the
Rio Grande watershed, is transitional
between the wetter northern headwaters of
the Rio Grande in Colorado and the arid
pine-oak forests in the headwaters of the
Rio Conchos in Mexico.

Maguey, Mimbres Mountains

Maguey, which is also called agave and
century plant, is a member of the Amaryllis
family. Its presence indicates desert
encroachment as the climate grows drier.

Sunrise on El Capitan, Guadalupe Mountains

These mountains, in Trans-Pecos Texas, rise between the Rio Grande and the Pecos River. They are composed of limestone and sandstone deposited in reef formations that grew in Permian seas hundreds of millions of years ago, before the Rocky Mountains were uplifted.

Headwaters of the Rio San Ignacio, Sierra Madre Occidental

This stream, flowing over polished volcanic bedrock, is one of the main tributaries of the Rio Conchos, sister source of the Rio Grande.

Frost on short grass and wild buckwheat,
headwaters of the Rio Conchos

This vegetation grows in the remnant
native grasslands of the high Mexican
plateau. Although the area has been
heavily grazed, it is said that the best
rangeland in northern Mexico once
occupied this area.

Pine-oak forest, upper canyon
of the Rio San Ignacio

The clearings in the forest mark the dwelling places of Tarahumara Indians, who live in isolated villages in the mountains of northern Mexico.

Volcanic streambed of the Rio Bocoyna

Short grass and pines grow on the eroded
ash that forms the river's banks.

*Red-capped lichens and pine needles
by the Rio Bocoyna*

The lichens are feeding on the volcanic
rock of the highlands, converting it to new
soil, which the decaying pine needles will
further enrich.

Upper gorge of the Rio San Juanito, Sierra Madre Occidental

Near the crest of the continental divide, called the Divisidero in Mexico, the Rio San Juanito meets the Rio Bocoyna, the Rio San Ignacio, and several lesser streams to form the Rio Conchos.

Braided sand by a spring on the
Rio Conchos

The blue strands are magnetite; the brown,
quartz sand. As the spring flows through
the sands, it sorts out the minerals on the
basis of weight, spinning out the lighter
ones from the heavier ones into a braided
pattern. On a minute scale, the spring
performs just as a river does at its delta
when it dumps its load of sediment into
the ocean.

Cobble bar on the Rio Conchos

On the horizon is the Sierra Grande,
the last major mountain range the Rio
Conchos has to cross before it reaches the
Rio Grande at Ojinaga, about twenty
miles away.

The crest of Sierra Grande, looking into Peguis Canyon

The Rio Conchos is carving through the last barrier before it enters the Presidio Bolson. It was in this great basin that the Rio Grande found its way into the older watershed of the Rio Conchos.

Peguis Canyon

Peguis Canyon, which is also known as
Boca Grande, is limestone that was
compressed more than most limestones, to
the extent that it almost metamorphosed
into marble. Short in distance—ten to
twelve miles—but Dantesque in magnitude,
Peguis is one of the most beautiful, and
certainly the wildest, of all the canyons in
the Rio Grande system.

Sculptured limestone in Peguis Canyon

Sand spilling from one depression to
another in the bedrock beside the Rio
Conchos shows in microcosm how the river
itself formed by filling a basin, spilling over,
cutting through a canyon, then flowing to
the next basin.

Red rain in Big Bend

Red rain—a rare sight, especially in the desert—occurs during storms just for a few minutes after sundown as the red rays shine through the top of the atmosphere.

Rainbow in waterfall mist

This waterfall, a paradisal anomaly in the desert, is on a side creek of the Rio Grande in the Presidio Bolson of Trans-Pecos Texas.

The Rio Grande in Colorado Canyon

The river has threaded its way through
massive layers of volcanic rock on the flanks
of the nearby Bofecillos Mountains. The
river is blue because it is winter, and the
low water carries very little sediment at
that season.

Cactus and bull muhly grass on the South Rim of the Chisos Mountains

The South Rim looks across the Sierra Quemada, or Burned Mountains, and the Rio Grande into Mexico.

Ocotillo, acacia, and mesquite on igneous rock

Ocotillo produces flowers first; then, if sufficient rain falls, leaves appear. All three plants are well armed with hooks, claws, and spines.

Reflections on flood mud in Santa Elena Canyon

As floodwater recedes, it loses its power to carry sediments. These cast-off deposits build up along the river, forming sandbars.

132

Mariscal Canyon

Bermuda grass and thick stands of giant
cane line the Rio Grande today. Photographs
from a hundred years ago show very little
riverside vegetation. Possibly, now that
there are several dams along the river, fewer
giant floods sweep away the vegetation
and soil.

Sunset on the Sierra del Carmen from Boquillas Canyon

Every clear evening the sun turns the cliffs of the Del Carmens deeper shades of rose. The pink cast results from the amount of iron in the limestone rocks.

*The Lower Canyons downstream
from La Linda*

The plant in the foreground is leatherstem,
shifting now into autumn colors. It is also
called blood of the dragon for the red
droplets that ooze from the plant when a
root is broken. The astringent drops are a
folk remedy for canker sores, fever blisters,
and other mouth ailments.

Hot Springs Rapid

This obstacle course of limestone boulders, discharged from the Arroyo San Rosendo, is one of the six biggest rapids in the Lower Canyons.

The Rio Grande below Burro Bluff

The cliffs here are more than a thousand feet high. Coming in on the far side of the river is Tule Canyon. It is the channel of an old, dead tributary that may once have equaled the current volume of the Rio Grande, but now it flash floods only periodically.

142

Razor rock limestone, near Langtry

Wild oregano, willow, and mesquite grow along the Rio Grande near its confluence with the Pecos River. In this region the river begins its transition from arid desert to subtropical plains.

Willow and bald cypress by the Rio Salado

A dense subtropical forest grows in the river valley along this Mexican tributary, which enters the Rio Grande above Falcon Reservoir.

Mesquite, prickly pear, and buffel grass

Below Falcon Reservoir the Rio Grande
cuts through one of the last remaining
patches of subtropical thorn forest in the
U.S. and adjacent Mexico.

Grassy islands in the Rio Grande

The flow of the river beyond Falcon
Reservoir is controlled by releases from the
spillway. At low water, islands crop up in
the river, places where herons, egrets,
cormorants, and ducks gather to feed and
rest. It is here also that the giant ringed
kingfisher perches on branches over the
water while hunting for fish.

Stepping-stones at Salineño

The boulders are ancient limestone
concretions, hardened masses in what was
probably a shallow ocean, bay, or estuary.
The river has since stripped away the
surrounding cover and exposed the rocks.
At this point the gradient is low, and the
Rio Grande is slowing down and widening,
no longer a youthful river.

Ancient seabed turned on end, near Monterrey

These peaks in the Sierra Madre Oriental are in the headwaters of the Rio Salinas, which joins the Rios Pesquira and San Juan before entering the Rio Grande below Laredo.

Folded limestone

Flat ocean bottom was upended when the Sierra Madre Oriental was uplifted. The yuccas on the cliff face, which grow to a height of about four feet, give some idea of the scale of the compressional forces that traveled through the rock.

Huasteca Canyon, near Monterrey

Within the desolate Sierra Madre Oriental,
pocket jungles occur in deep, narrow
canyons like Huasteca. Here temperate and
tropical vegetation—including a lead tree,
an Arizona pine, oaks, palms, and yuccas—
grow side by side on the limestone cliffs.

*Springs at the headwaters of the
Rio San Juan*

Polished boulders show the effects of flash
floods that roar down the narrow canyons
during summer thunderstorms.

The travertine cape of Horsetail Falls

In the Sierra Madre Oriental a lot of water
sinks underground into limestone caverns,
emerging finally in the foothills at big
springs—called *nacimientos* in Mexico. At
Horsetail Falls, on a tributary of the Rio
San Juan, water plunges over the last cliffs
in the range. Some water evaporates as it
cascades, leaving behind mineral deposits
that form the smooth travertine cape.

Tropical Spanish moss, oak, and desert agave in Huasteca Canyon

Tropical and arid vegetation share a transition zone between the high mountains and low desert.

Blades of Sabal texana

A tall, stout palm, *Sabal texana* once
occurred in dense stands near the Rio
Grande at the tip of Texas and throughout
northeastern Mexico. All but a few patches
have been cleared for agriculture, and now
fewer than a hundred scattered acres
remain in Texas. The largest stand is at the
National Audubon *Sabal* palm preserve just
south of Brownsville.

166

Tidal marshes below Palmetto Hill

Long-legged shorebirds—avocets and
possibly a willet—forage amid *Batis*, or
saltwort, in the shallow brackish waters of
the Rio Grande delta.

Spartina on Laguna Madre salt flats

A sea of hardy grass covers the shores of Laguna Madre, on both the mainland and the back side of Padre Island.

Beach primrose, railroad vine, and wind-blown spartina

These plants, along with sea oats, are the first stabilizers of the dunes. Together, like a huge web, they help trap sand and hold the dunes in place. The tiny tracks are from ghost crabs that scavenge inland from the shore.

Wind-rippled dunes, Padre Island

The dunes are made largely of sand that was emptied into the Gulf by the Rio Grande, then carried up along the coast on the long shore current, and finally washed ashore with shell fragments by the waves. The sand is composed of the resistant remains of rock, mostly quartz, that the Rio Grande could not pulverize or dissolve.

Gulf surf on Padre Island

Wind-generated waves continually roll
ashore, depositing sand that is then blown
into dunes.

Donax and sand dollars

A big Gulf storm heaved the multicolored donax clamshells ashore, where most of the colony probably perished. Mass die-offs of this sort occur in the geologic record as coquina limestone, compressed sediment densely packed with fossil shells.

Sunrise behind storm clouds at Boca Chica

The spit of land is the Mexican side of Boca Chica, the mouth of the Rio Grande. The river, flowing to the left in the foreground, is merging with the Gulf of Mexico. Water in the ocean evaporates, clouds rise, and the moisture enters a sort of atmospheric river that will carry it north over the mountains, where it will be released again as rain and snow and reenter the Rio Grande. The roots of the river are in the mountains; the source is in the sea. Boca Chica is both the end and the beginning of the Rio Grande.

ABOUT THE PHOTOGRAPHER

Jim Bones was born in Monroe, Louisiana, in 1943. His father was in the Air Force; hence Jim and his parents moved a great deal. As a child, he lived in Florida, Texas, California, Maryland, and Virginia. One Christmas when he was in junior high, his parents gave him a Brownie 8mm movie camera, and shortly thereafter they began a cross-country trip from one home, in Norfolk, Virginia, to another in Lompoc, California. It was on that trip that Jim developed an interest in both photography and the desert.

He started college at the University of Texas with the intention of studying aerospace engineering, took a semester of physics, then switched to geology. Toward the end of college he switched again to fine arts, primarily to study with and work for photographer Russell Lee, who is a master of large-format black and white documentary photography.

Since 1965 Bones has worked with a large-format (4x5) camera. He spent a year (1972–1973) at the Dobie-Paisano Ranch, near Austin, and the photographs he took during his residency there were published in 1975 in *Texas Heartland: A Hill Country Year*. From 1975 to 1978 he worked in Santa Fe, New Mexico, as printing assistant to photographer Eliot Porter, who is widely respected for his large-format color work, especially of nature. Bones' other books include *Texas Earth Surfaces* (1970), *Texas Wild* (1976), and *Texas West of the Pecos* (1981). Encino Press of Austin, Texas, has published two portfolios of Bones' handmade dye-transfer prints, *A Texas Portfolio* (1977) and *A Wildflower Portfolio* (1978).

Jim Bones is also a writer and a wilderness guide who leads photographic tours through his own company. His home base is Santa Fe, but for the last twenty or so years he has spent a good bit of his time afield in the watershed of the Rio Grande.